Stress Relieving
HIPPIE ROCKERS
Rock Coloring Book

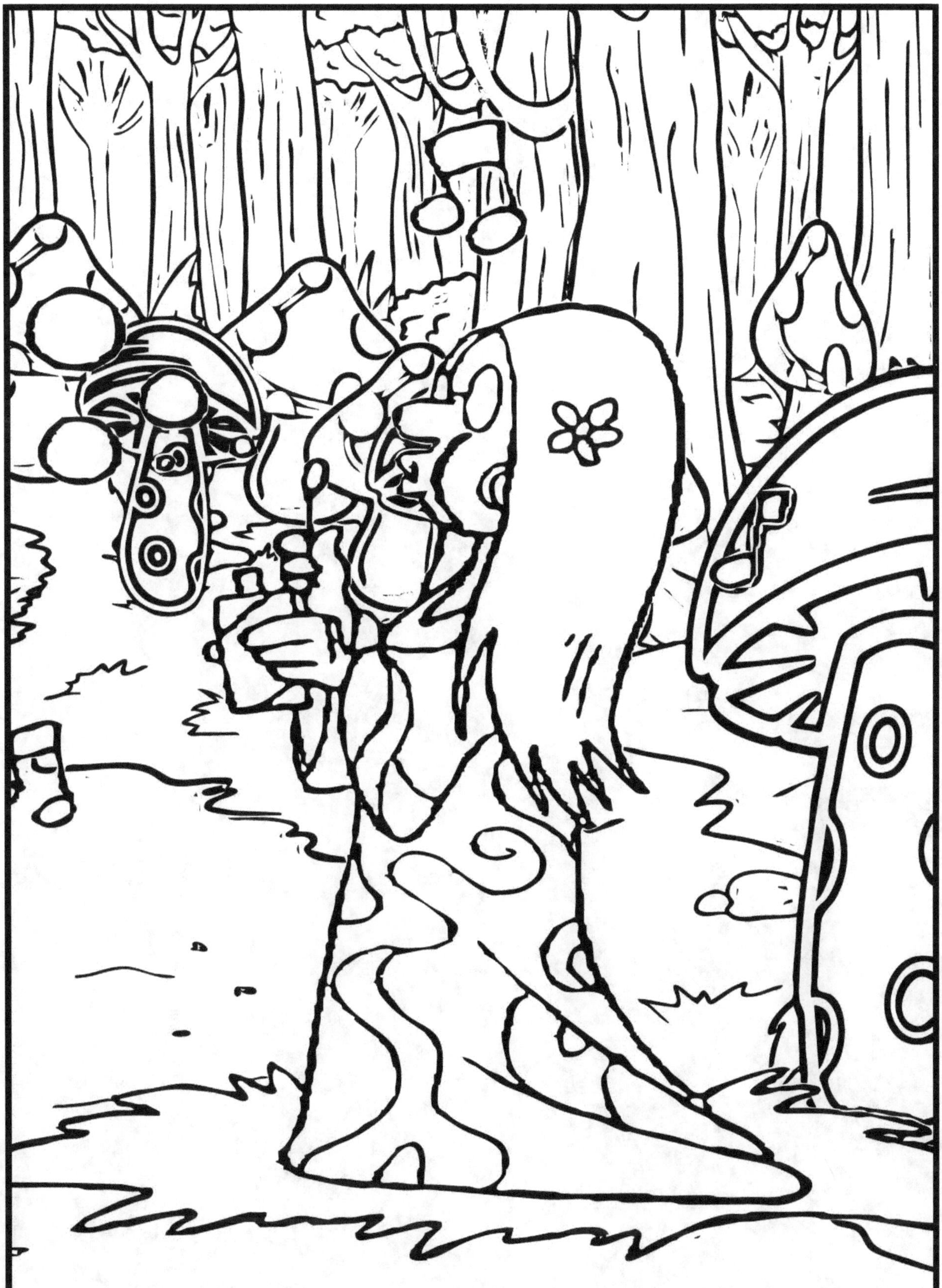

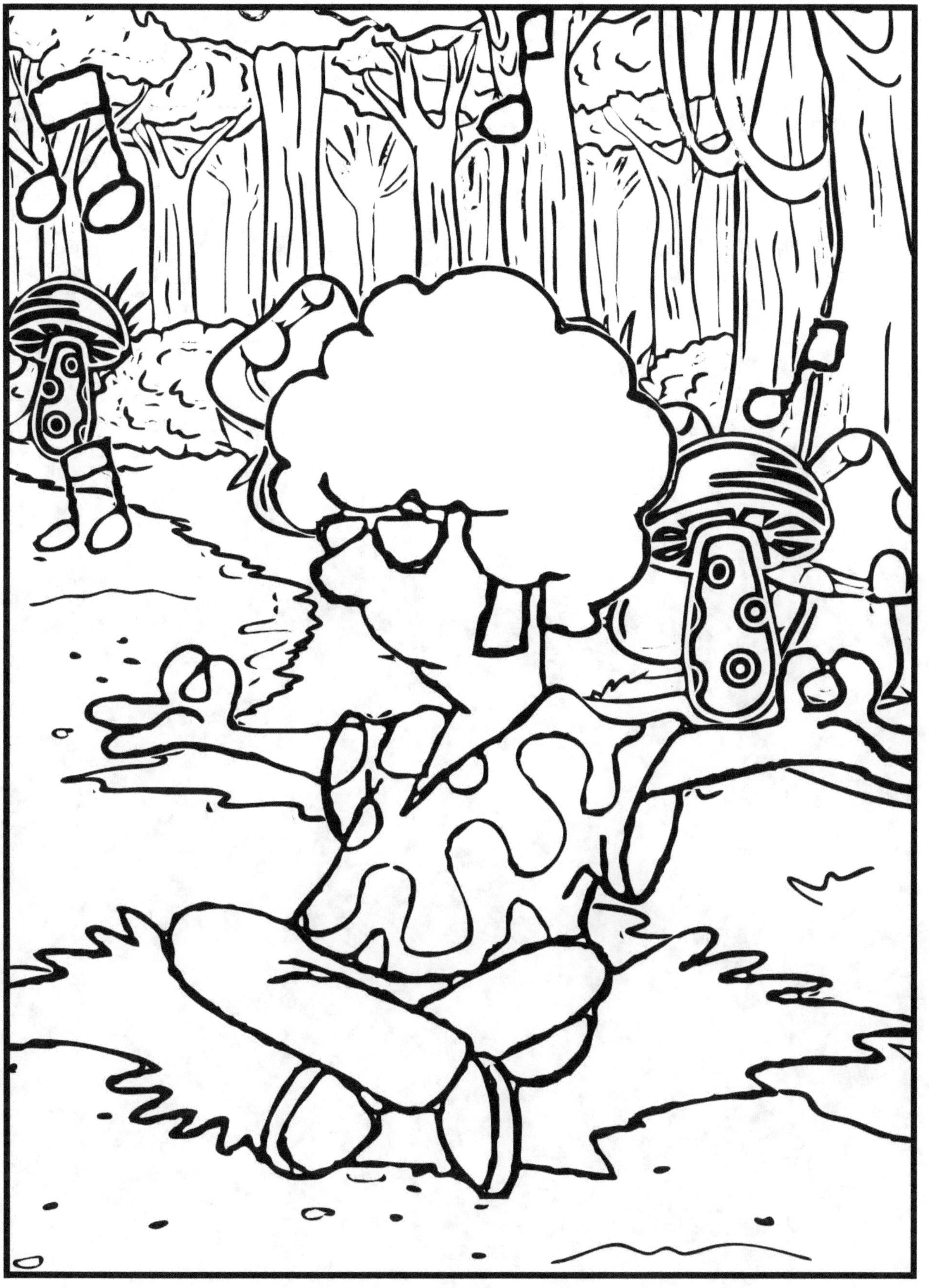

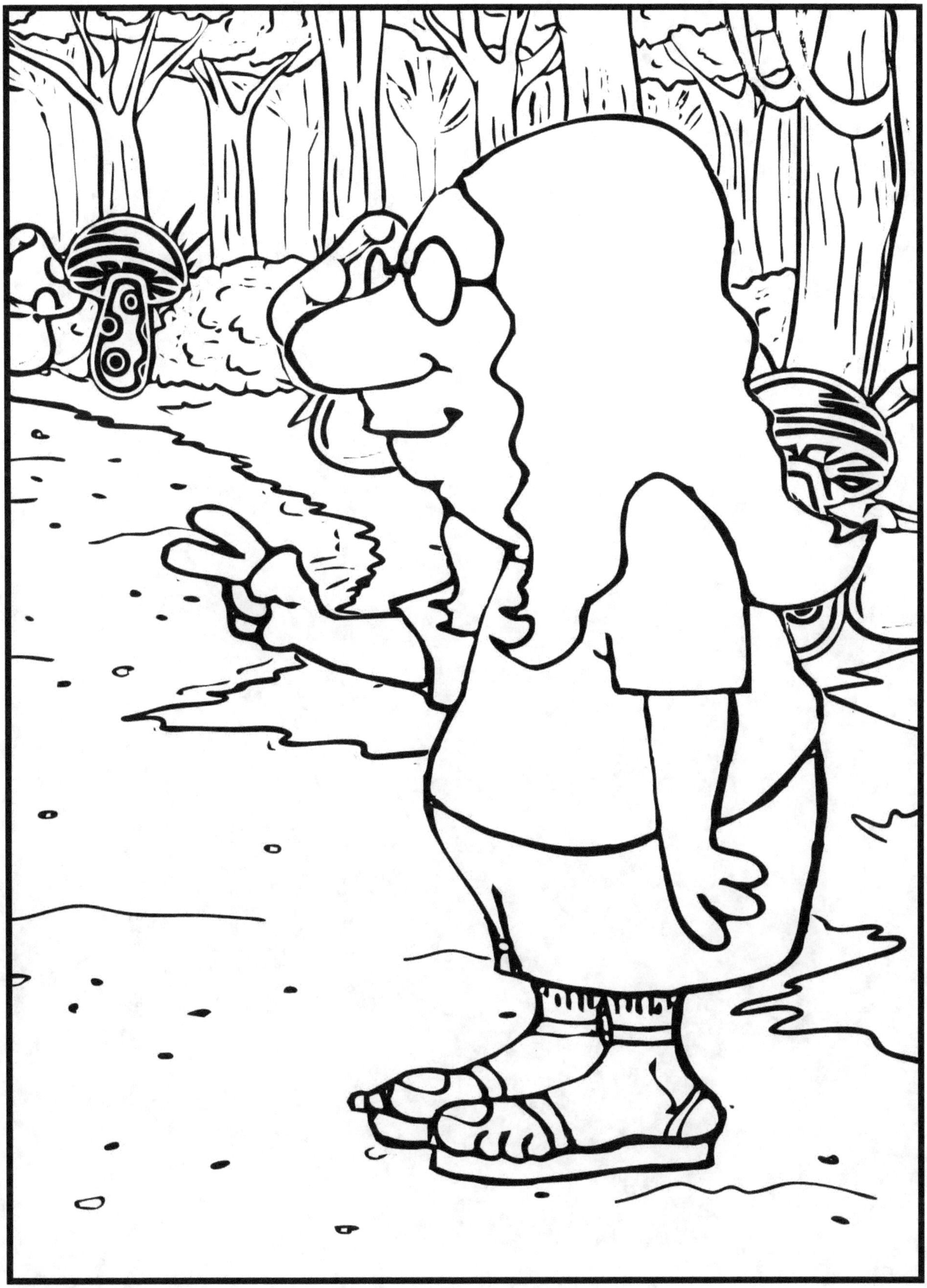

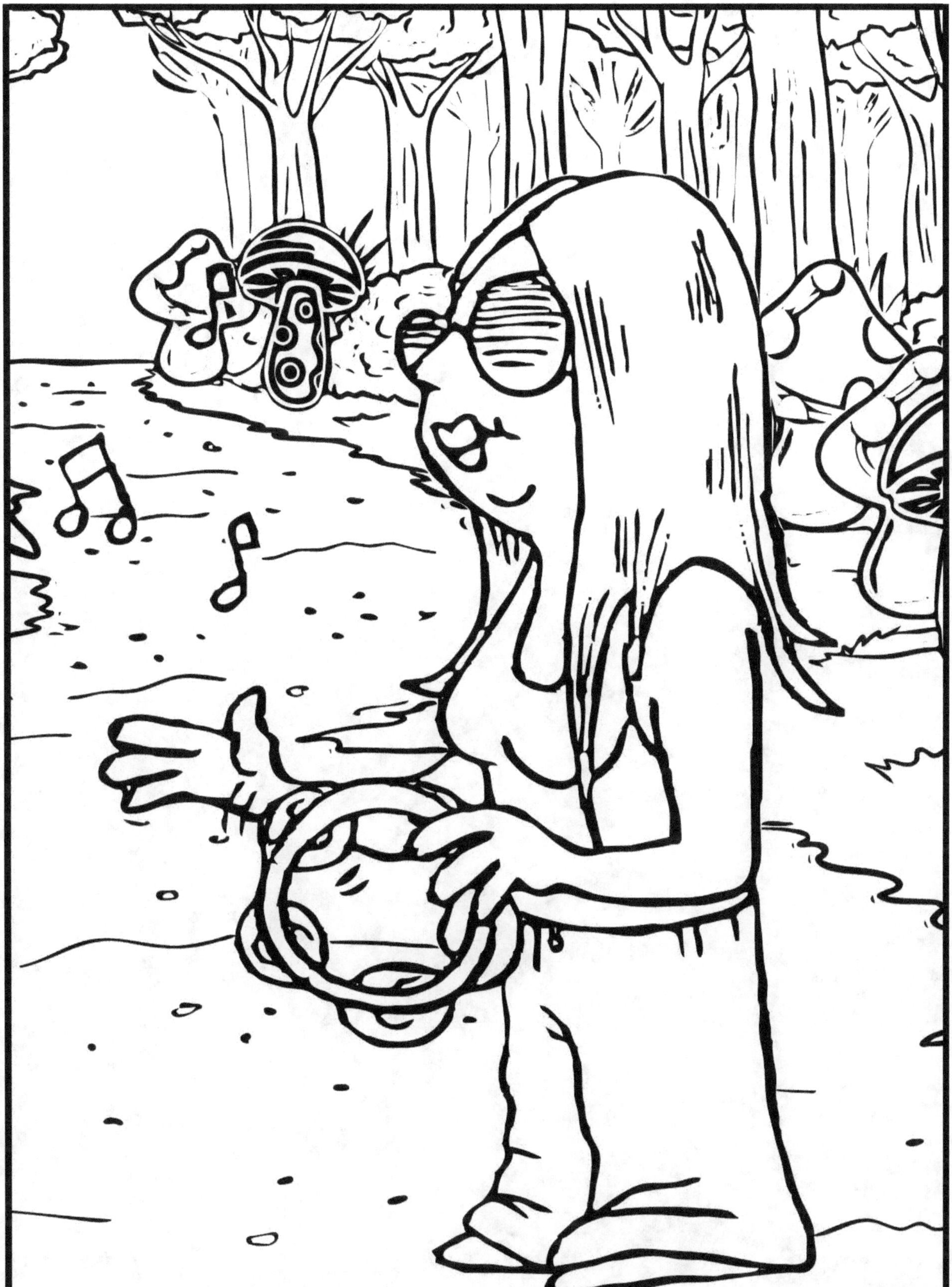

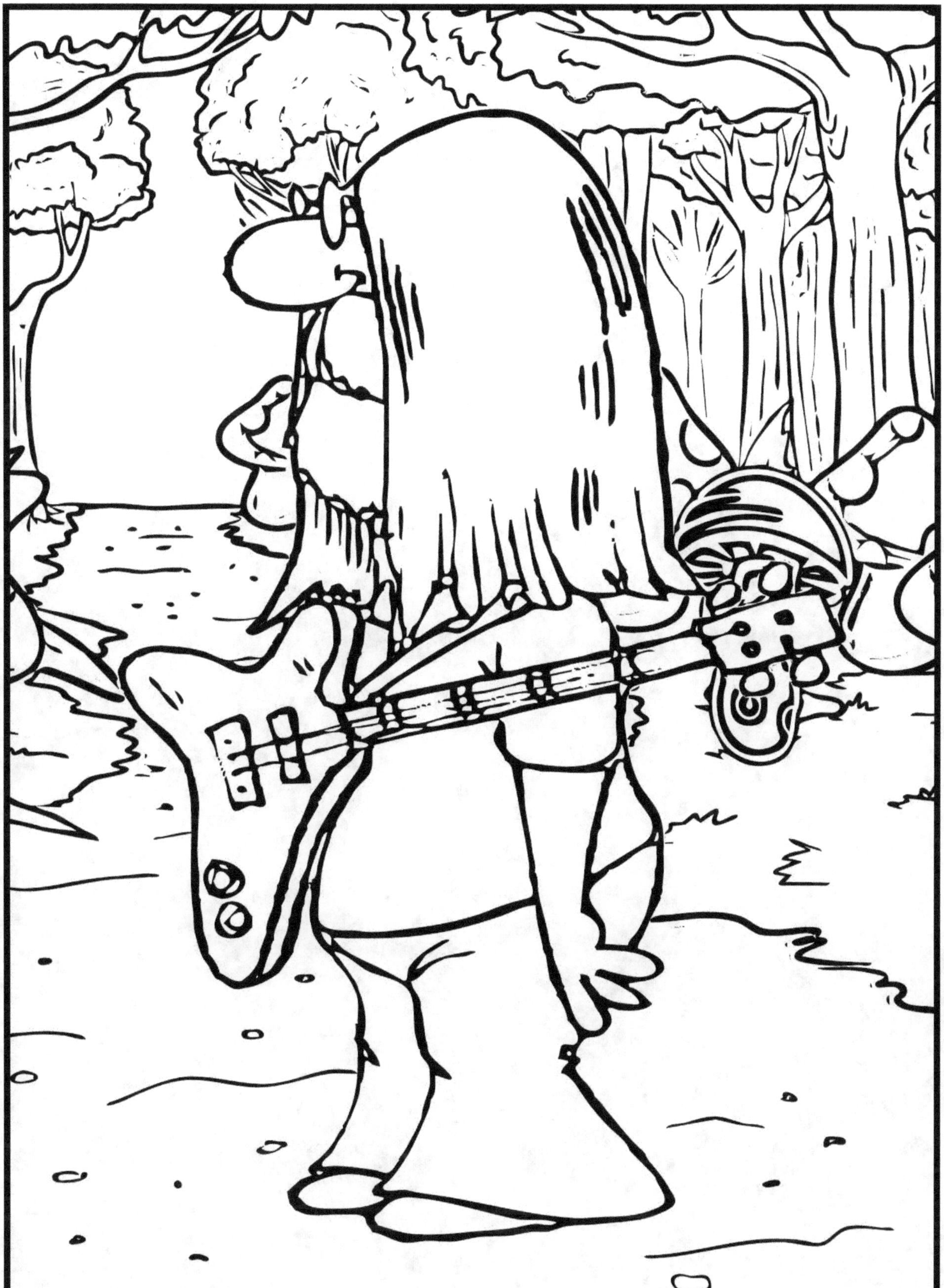

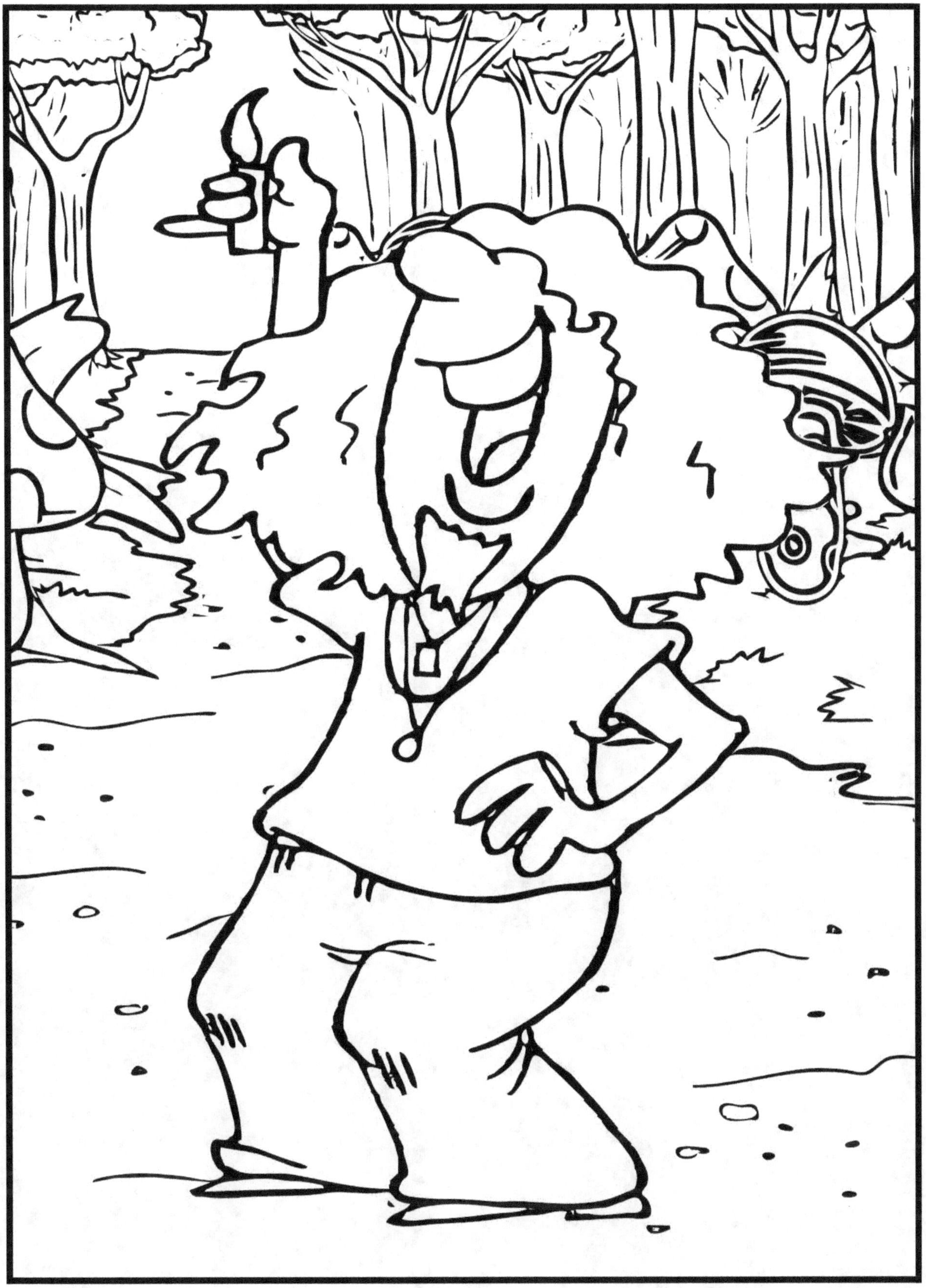

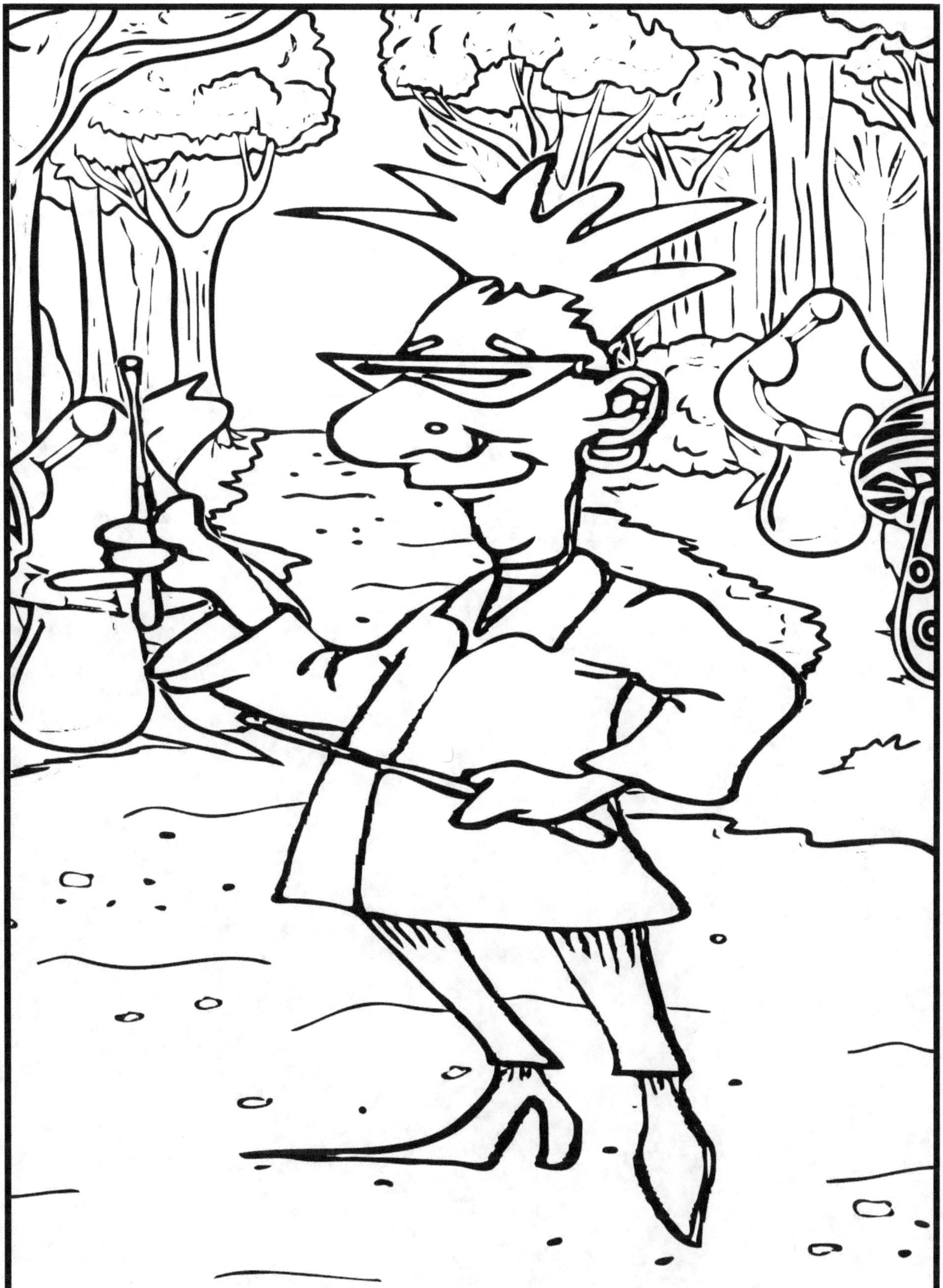

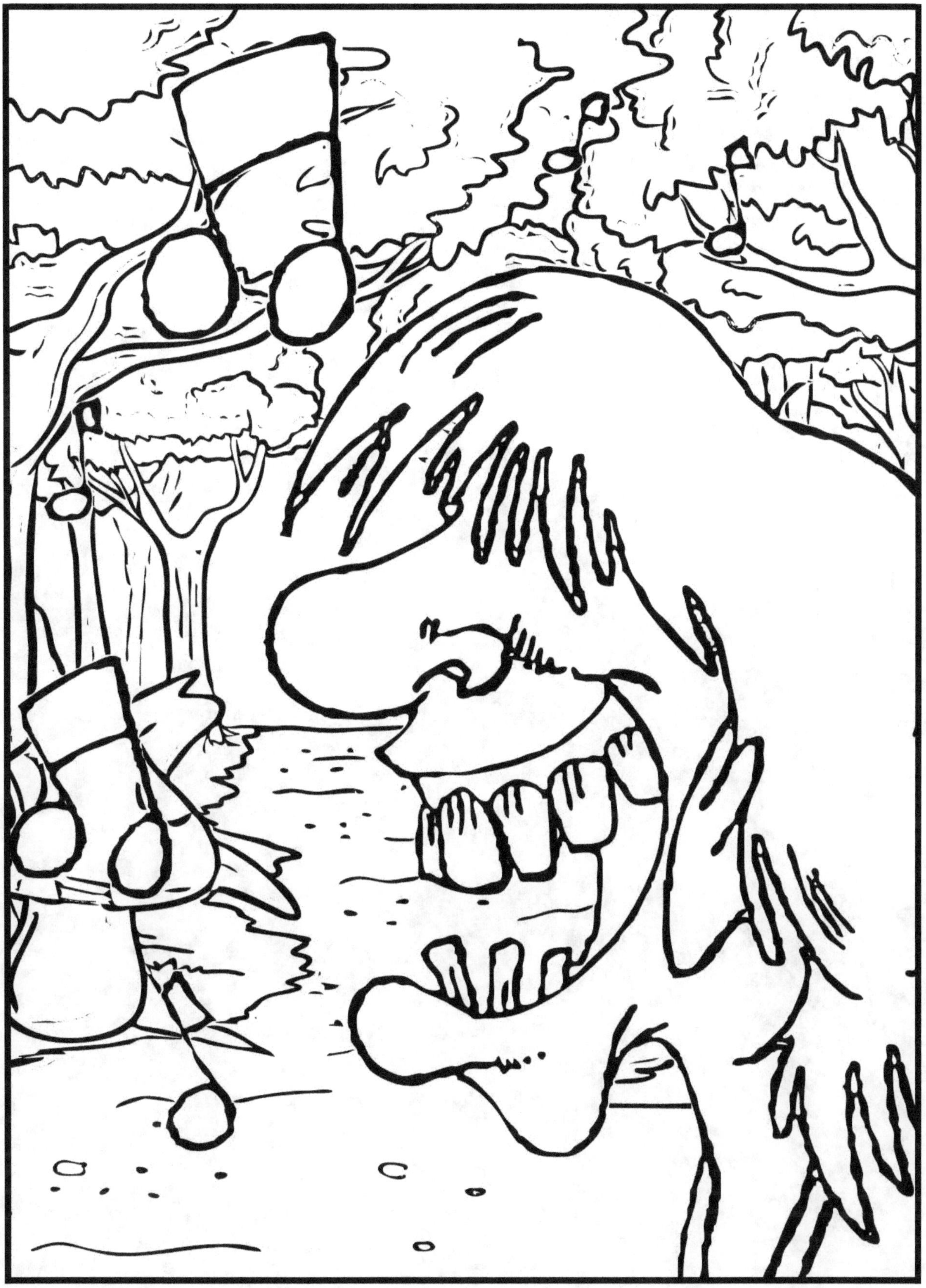

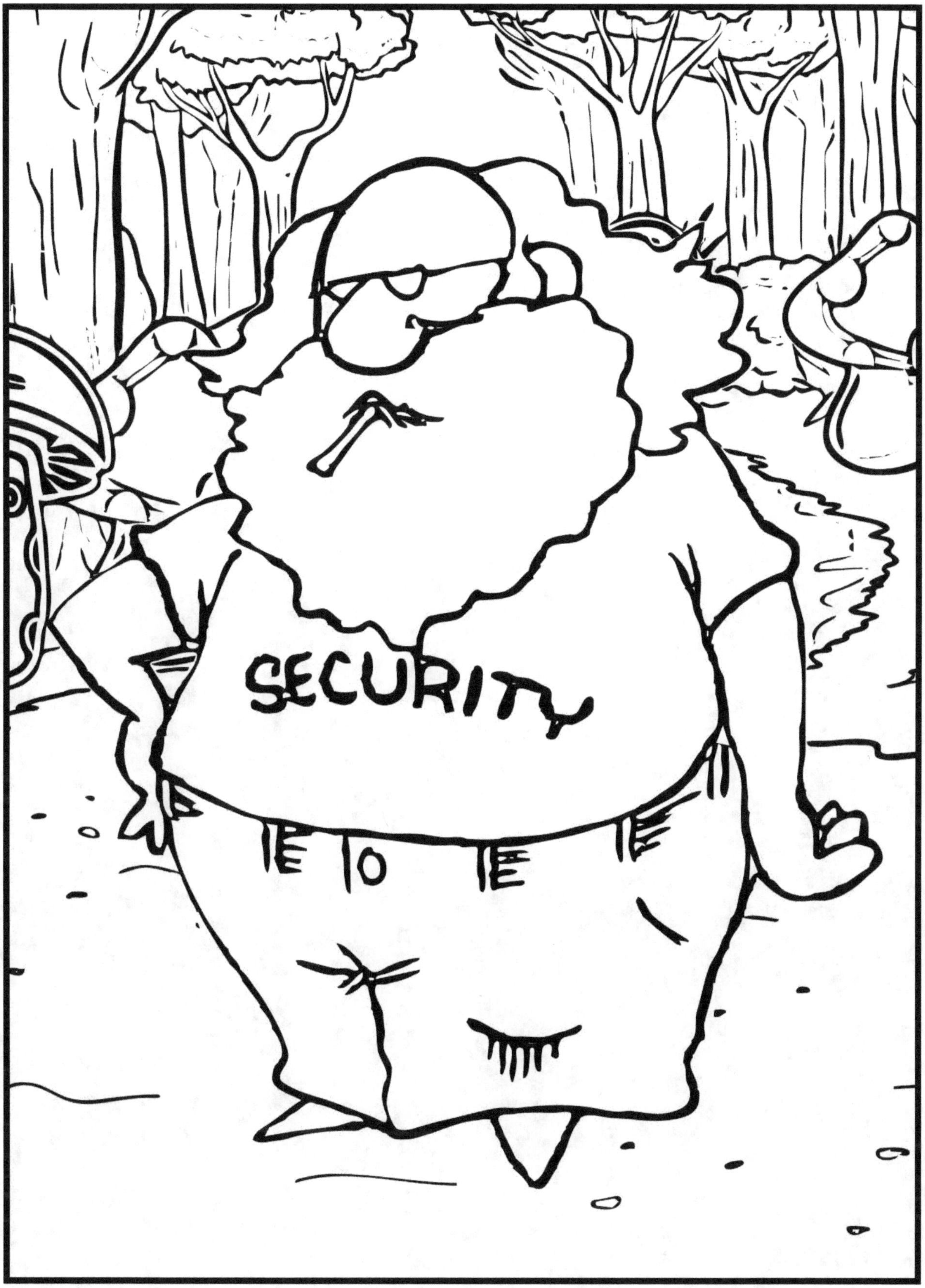
SECURITY

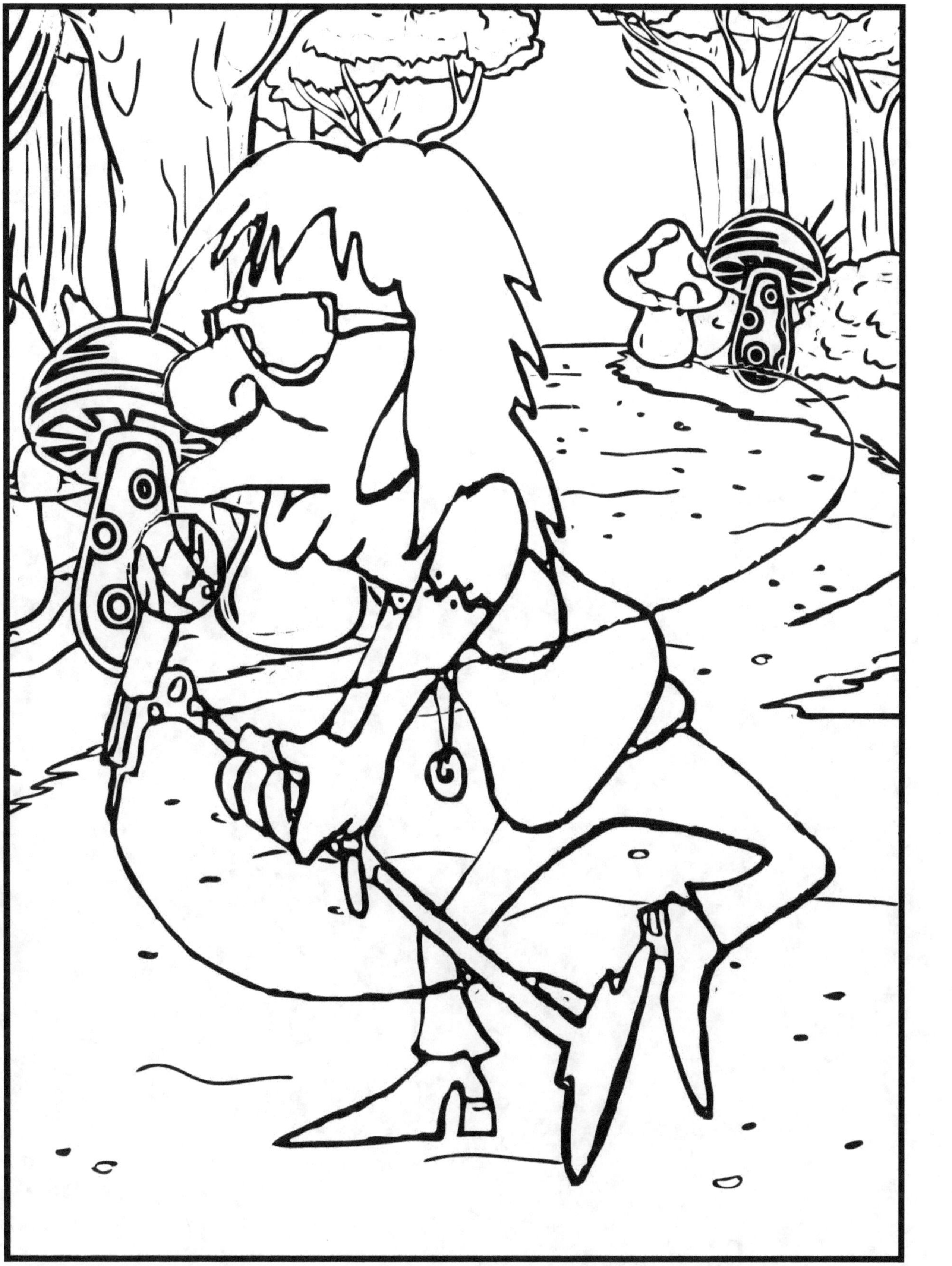

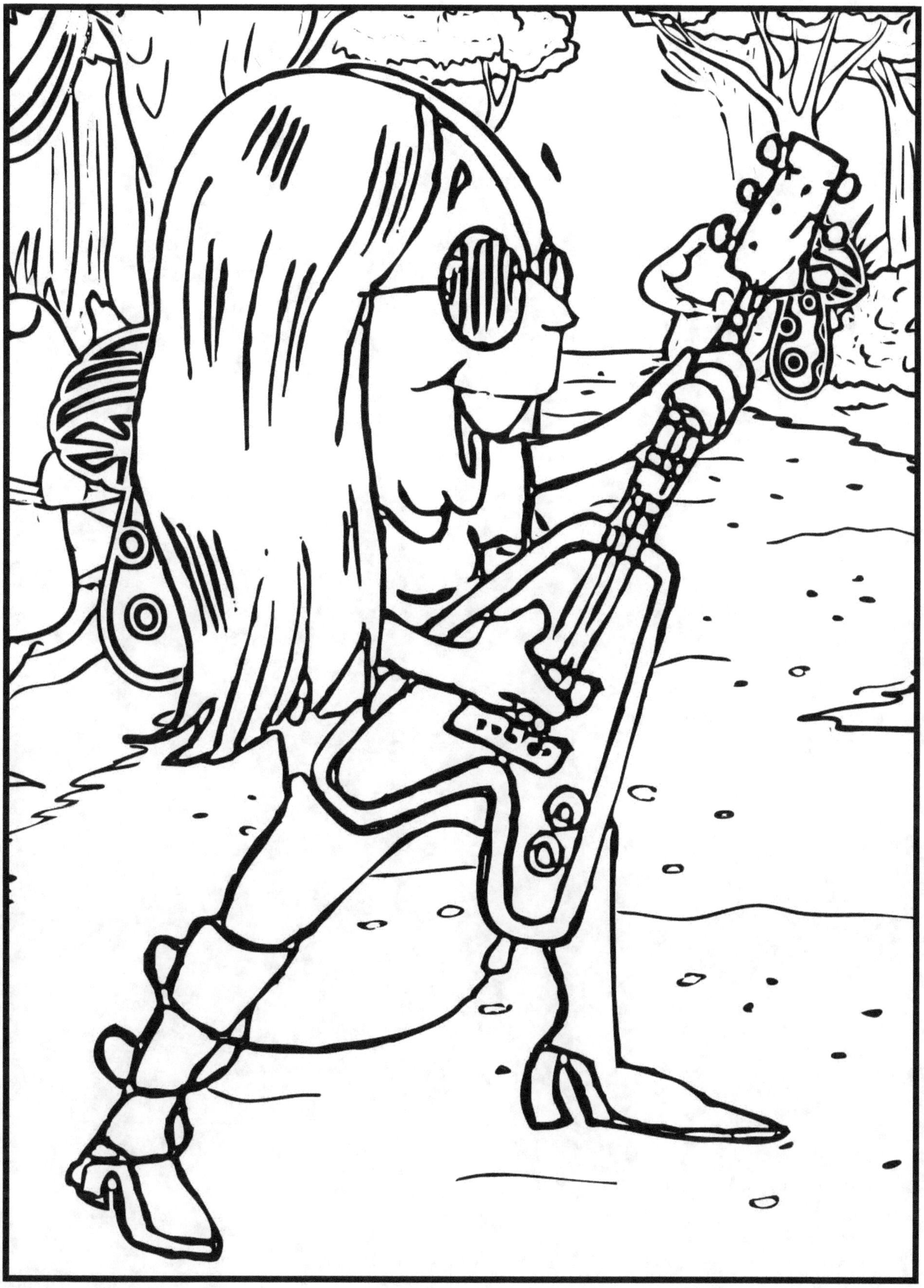

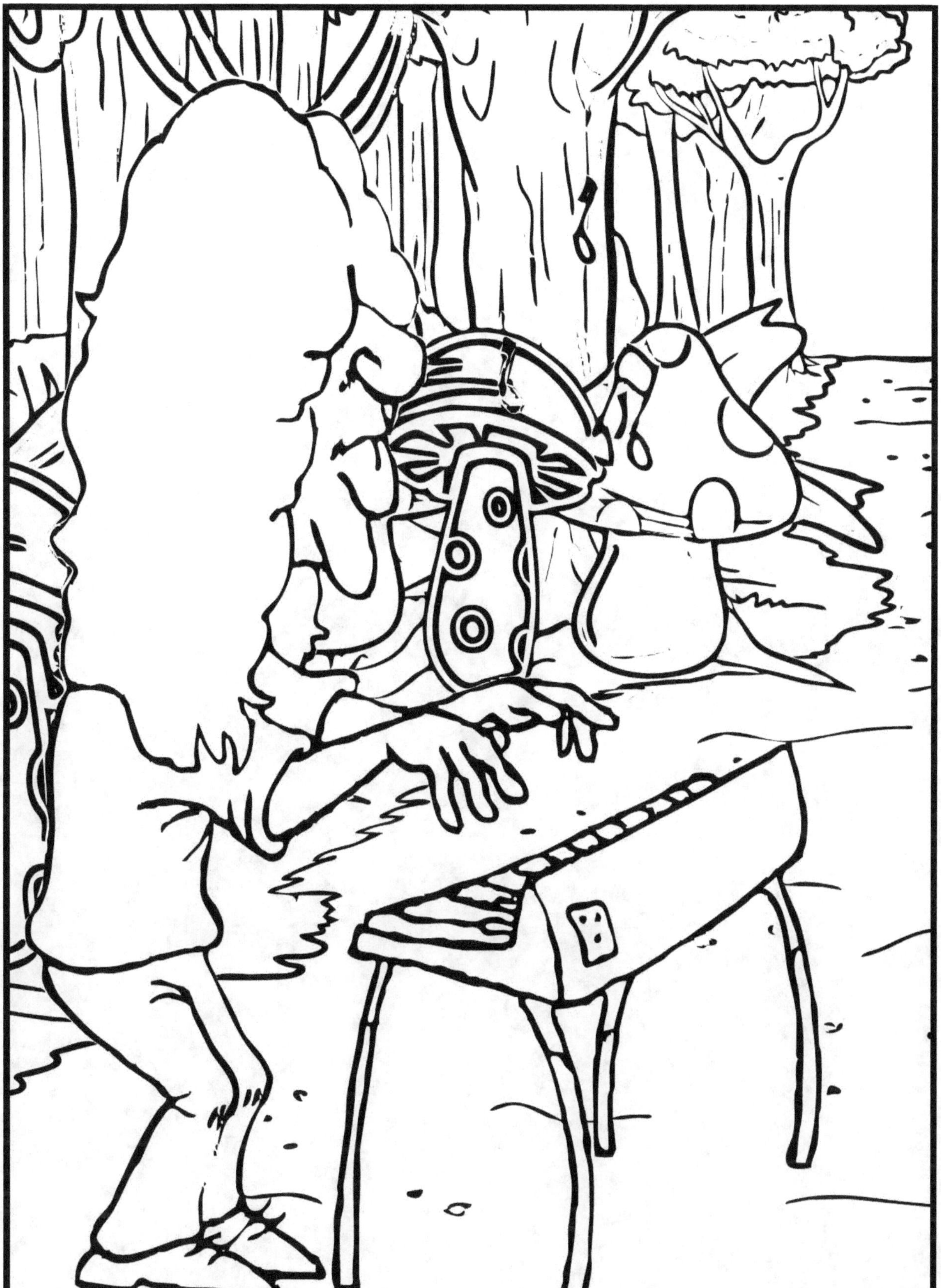

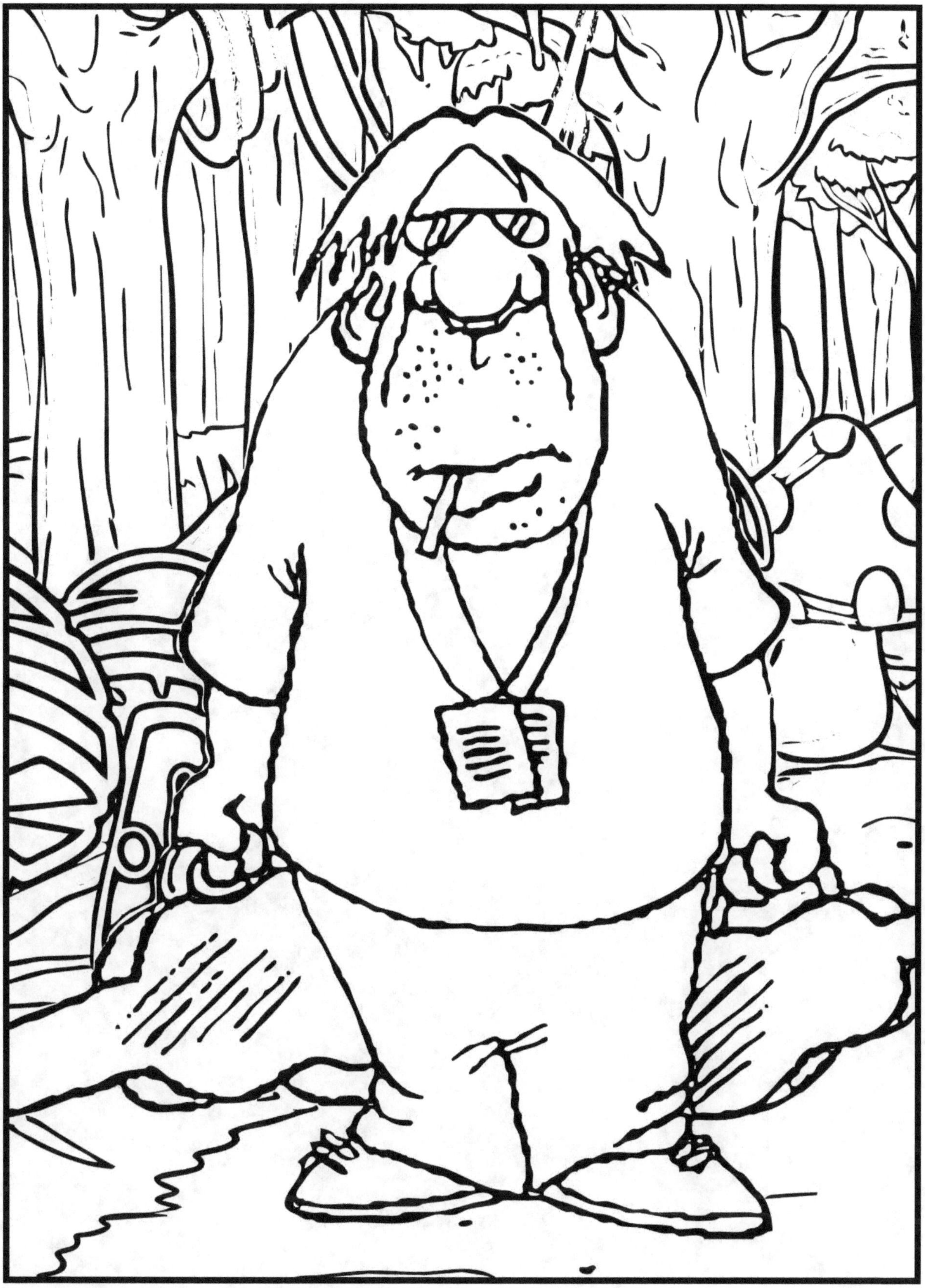

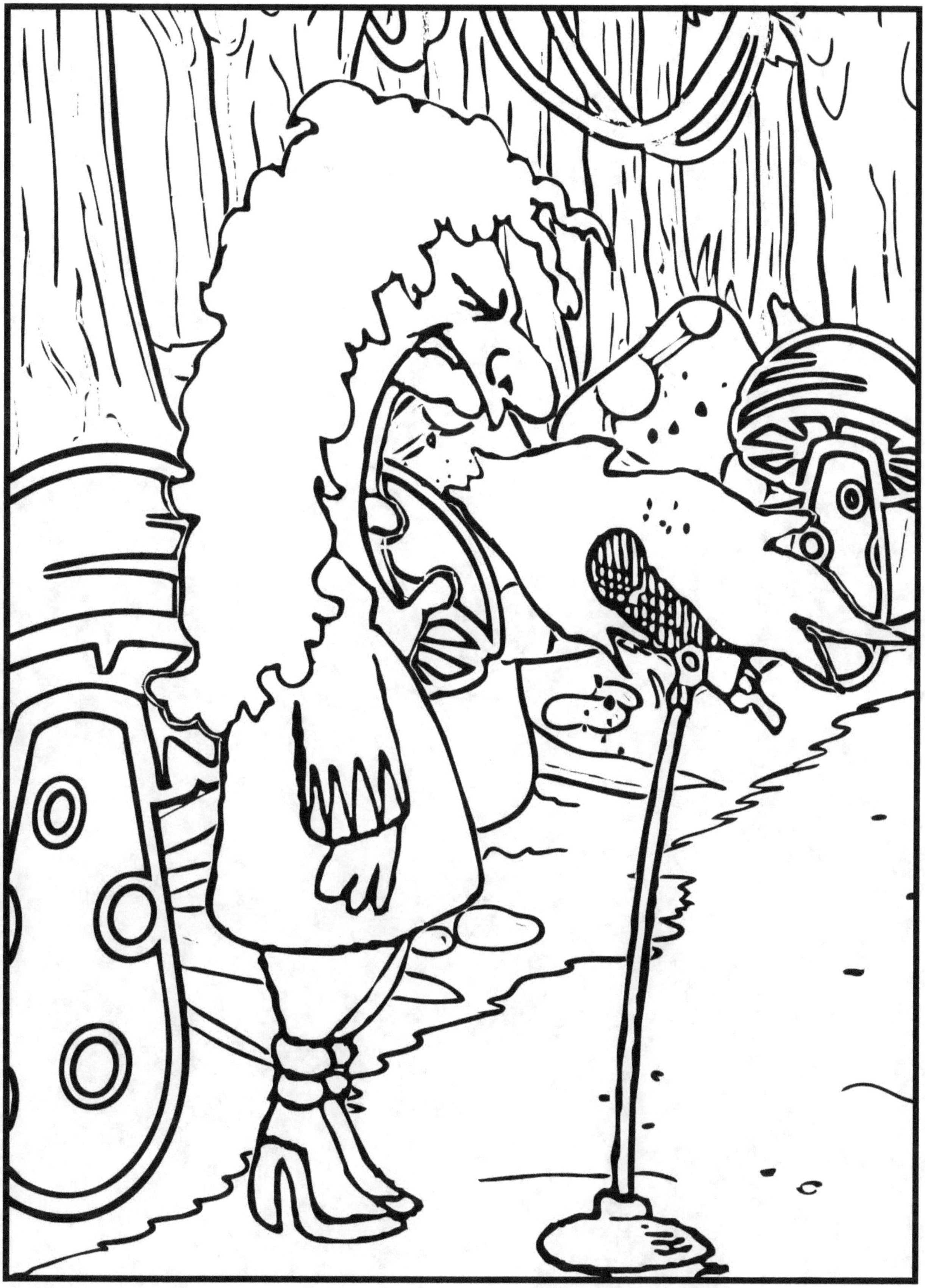

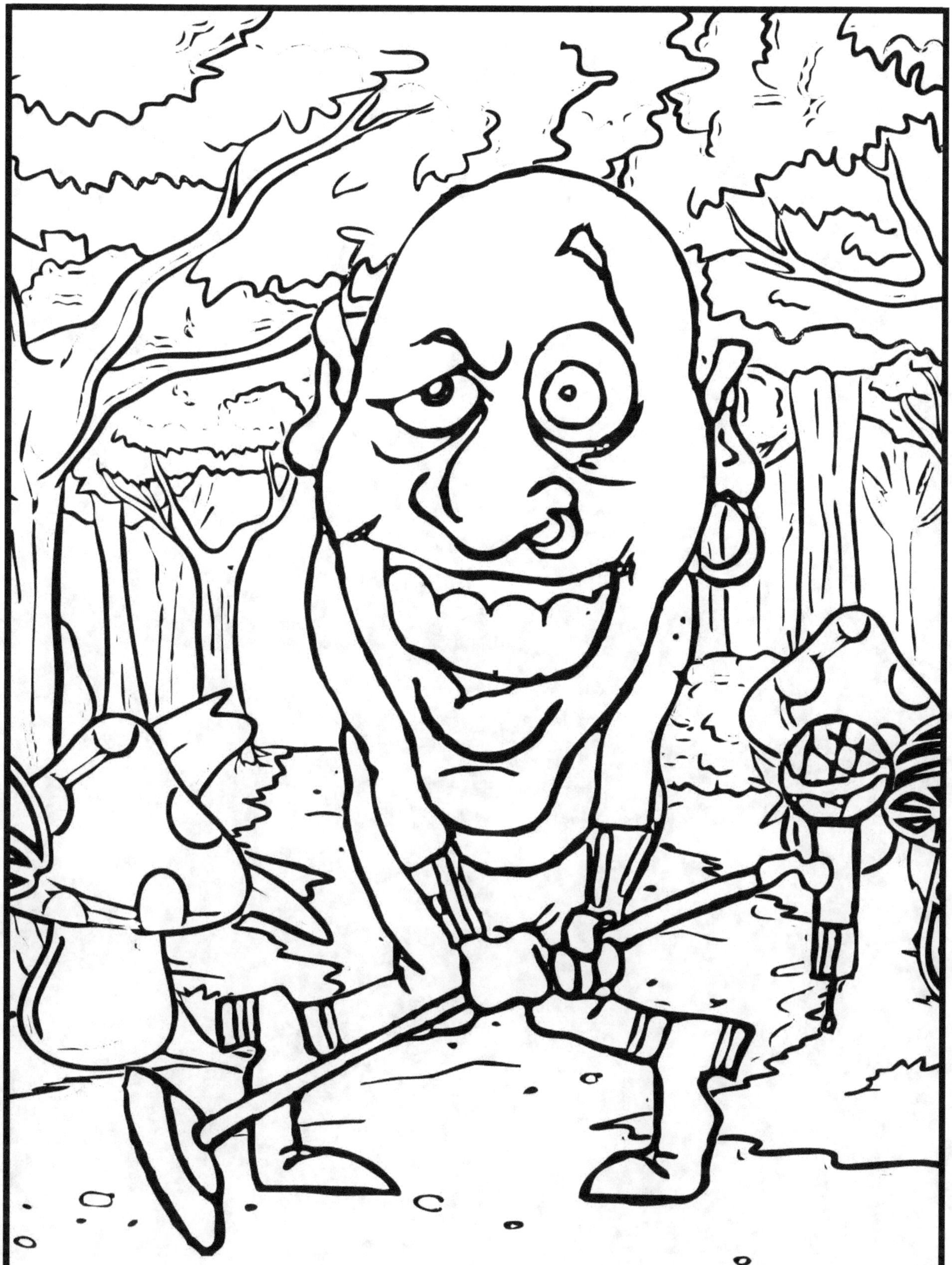

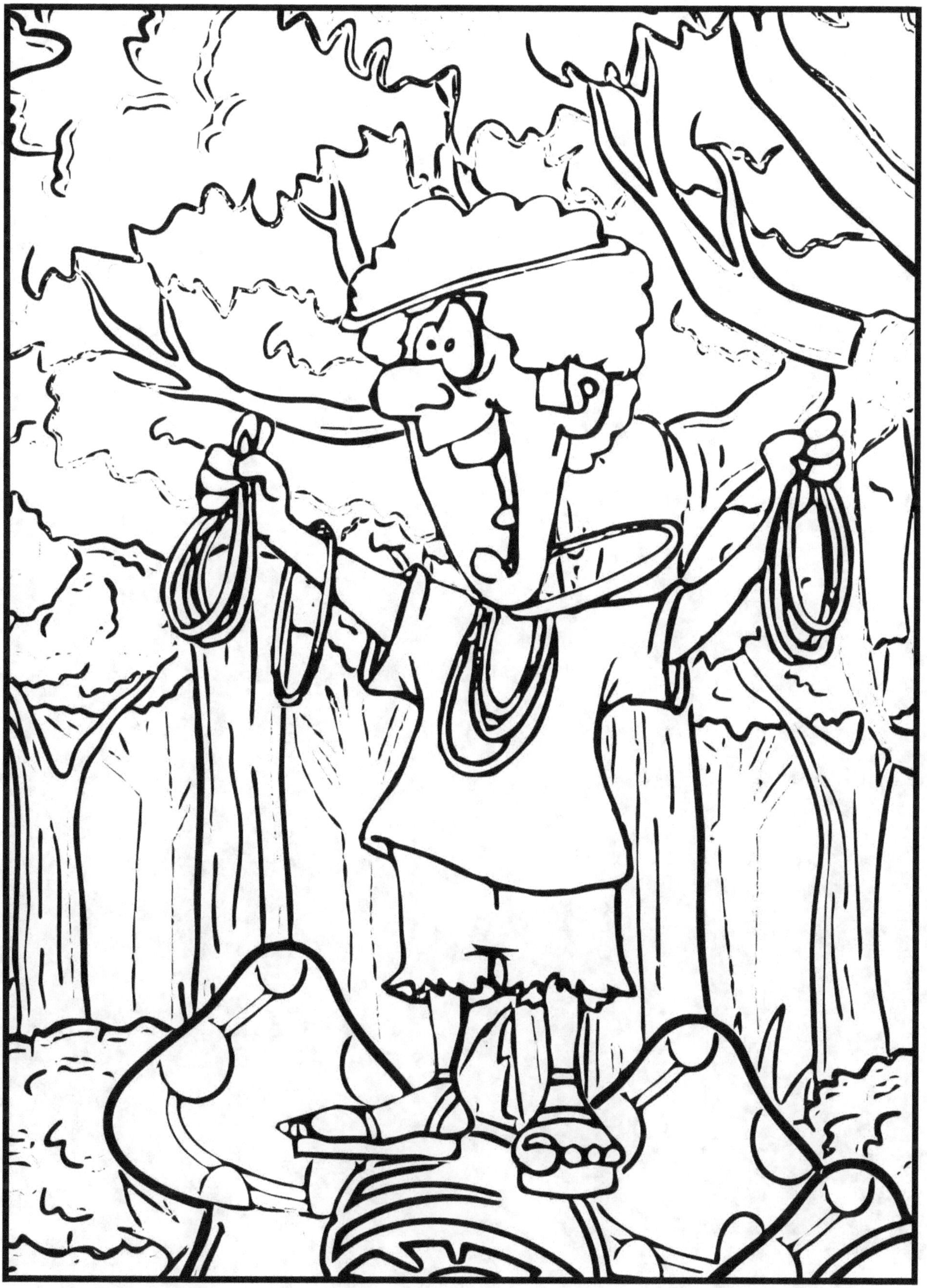

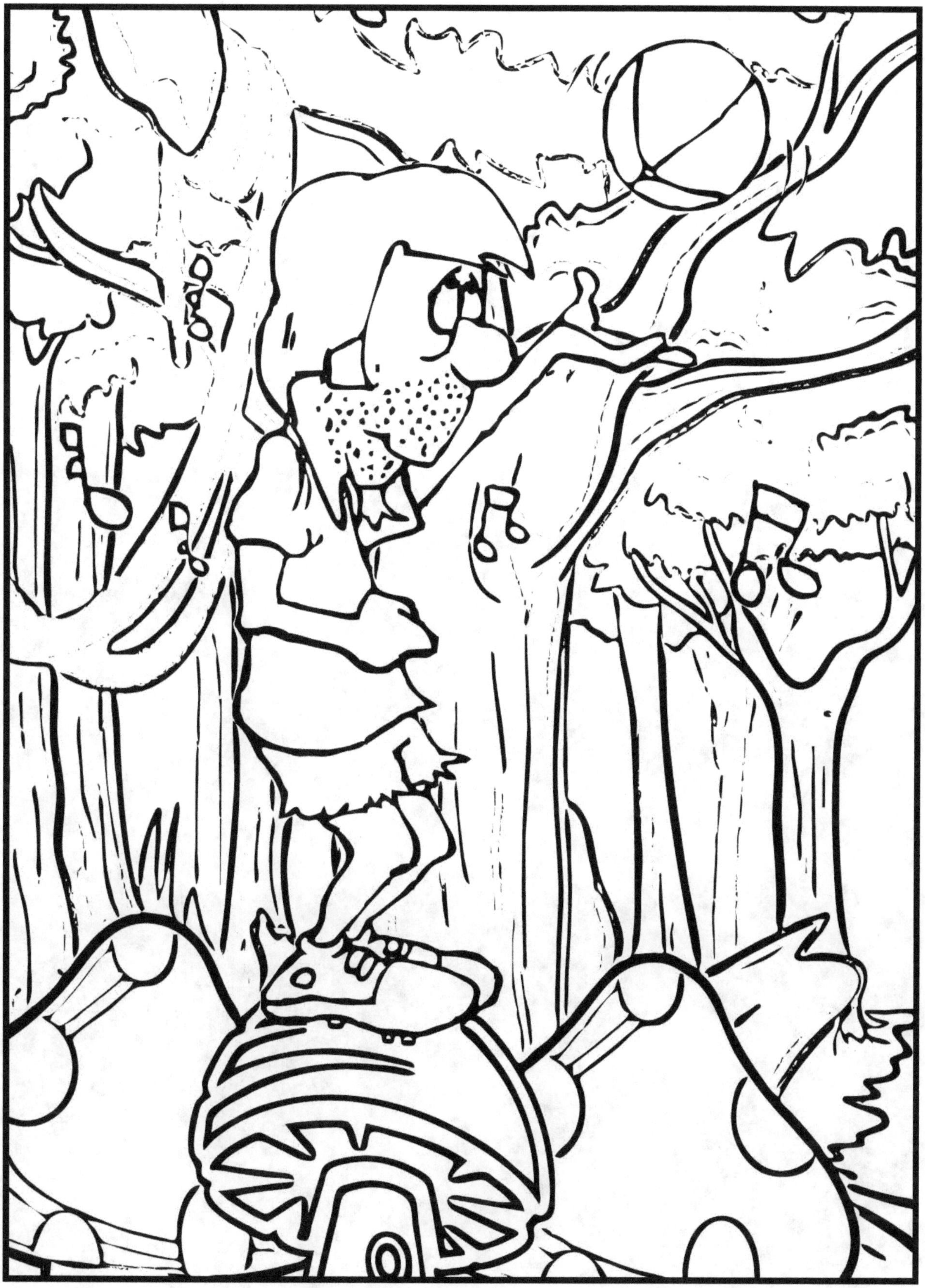

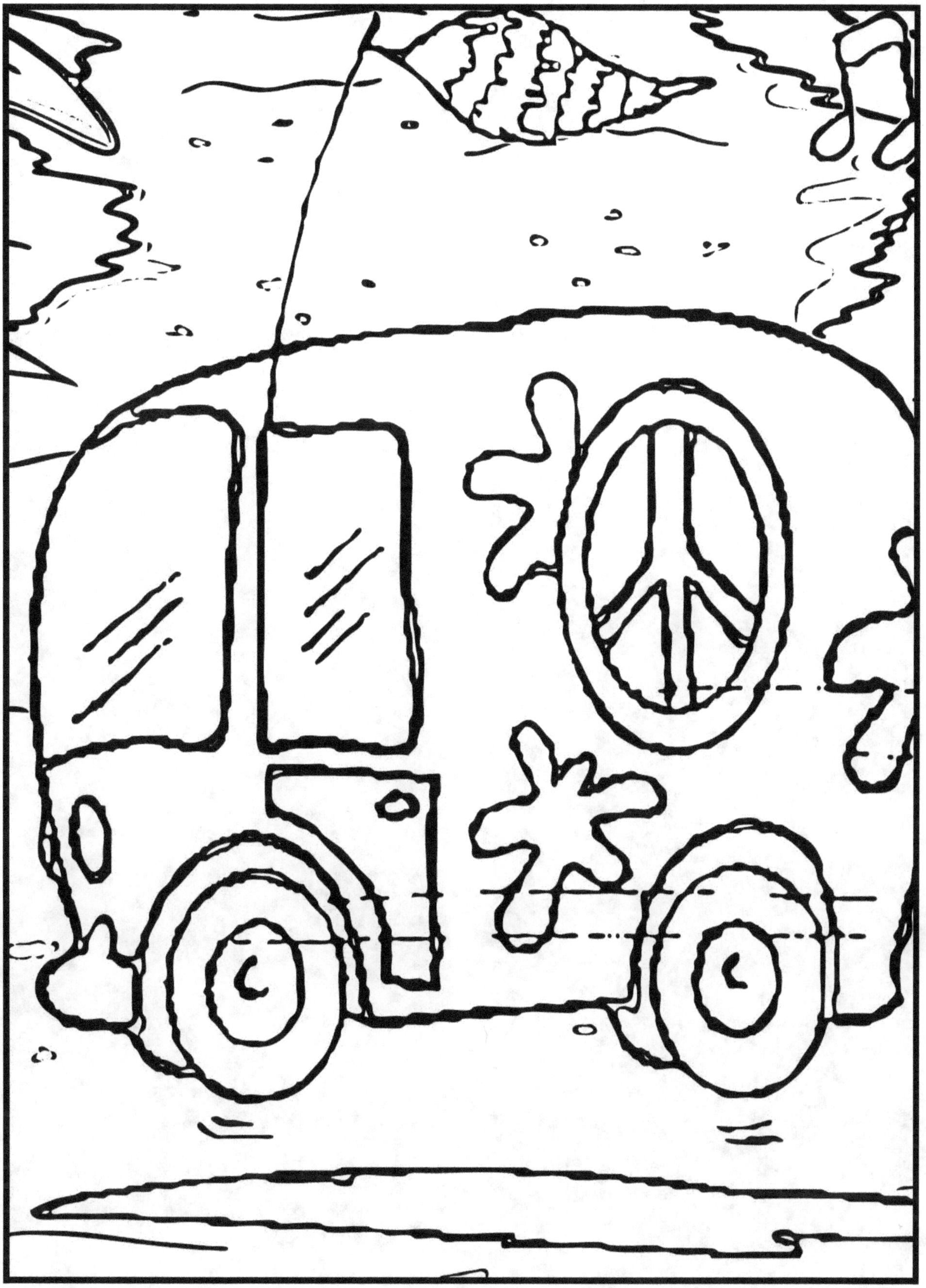

www.ingramcontent.com/pod-product-compliance
Lightning Source LLC
Chambersburg PA
CBHW081406170526
45166CB00010B/3232
* 9 7 8 1 5 1 9 6 4 8 8 3 9 *